Threads of Feeling

FOUNDLING

Letter *Male*

Threads of Feeling

THE LONDON FOUNDLING HOSPITAL'S TEXTILE TOKENS, 1740–1770

John Styles

ISBN 978 0 955180 85 9

British Library Cataloguing in Publication Data
A catalogue record of this book is available from the British Library

Design by Laura Parker

Printed by Synergie Group, UK

COVER: 'The Bit of Red Cloth Enclosed was pined to the Childs Cap': a heart
cut from red woollen cloth, a ribbon of blue paduasoy silk, and a piece of linen
diaper. Foundling 10563, a girl admitted 22 November 1758

FRONTISPIECE: 'Striped camblet'. Foundling 10875, a boy admitted 16
December 1758

Arts & Humanities
Research Council

IMAGE COPYRIGHT

Cover, frontispiece, figs. 1–6, 8–21, 23–30, 32–35, 37–38, 41–43, 45–47, 49–60:
© Coram; figs. 7, 39, 44: The Foundling Museum; fig. 22: ©NTPL/Andreas
von Einsiedel; figs. 31, 48: Courtesy of The Lewis Walpole Library, Yale
University; fig. 36: Manuscripts, Archives and Special Collections, Washington
State University Libraries, PN1376.S53; fig. 40: By courtesy of the Trustees of Sir
John Soane's Museum

CONTENTS

6   Preface

8   Introduction

10   1. The Foundling Hospital and its Tokens

18   2. Textiles

30   3. Fashion

42   4. Ribbons

52   5. Baby clothes

56   6. Needlework

62   7. Mothers and Babies

70   Conclusion

72   Select Bibliography

PREFACE

I FIRST REALIZED THE IMPORTANCE of the Foundling Hospital's collection of eighteenth-century textiles as I researched ordinary people's clothing for my book *The Dress of the People: Everyday Fashion in Eighteenth-Century England*, published in 2007. Very few pieces of eighteenth-century clothing have survived that can be identified with any confidence as having belonged to the poor. Ordinary people's clothes were worn and re-worn by a succession of owners until they fell into rags, or they were cut up and reused for quilts, baby clothes, and the like. If, by chance, they outlived the eighteenth century, they were unlikely to excite the attention of collectors or museums. Nineteenth- and twentieth-century museum collections of costume were built up primarily from the clothes worn by the rich, which had comprised the cutting edge of fashion. *The Dress of the People*, consequently, could make little use of surviving garments to provide evidence about the visual and material characteristics of eighteenth-century working people's clothing. In the absence of surviving clothing, I searched instead for surviving textiles. Historians of children's clothing pointed me to the Foundling Textiles. As I sifted through some 5,000 rare, beautiful, mundane and moving scraps of fabric, I knew I had at last found my archive – Britain's largest collection of everyday textiles. They had so much to tell us, not just about the history of fabric and clothing, but also about the lives of poor women and their babies, yet they were virtually unknown beyond a small coterie of specialists. Out of that realization came the idea for this book and its accompanying exhibition at the Foundling Museum.

Neither the book nor the exhibition would have been possible without the enthusiasm and hard work of the staff at the Foundling

Museum and London Metropolitan Archives. I am particularly grateful to Rhian Harris, Lars Tharp and Michael Parker for their support. I owe a special debt of gratitude to two of the Museum's volunteers, Gillian Clark and Janette Bright, both experts on different aspects of eighteenth-century clothing and textiles. They have been unfailingly generous in sharing their research into the Foundling tokens with me. Coram, the children's charity that owns the Foundling Hospital records, enthusiastically supported the book and the exhibition. I would not have had time to complete either without a Knowledge Transfer Fellowship from the Arts and Humanities Research Council. Laura Parker demonstrated an impressive combination of generosity, skill and patience in designing the book under pressure. And finally I must acknowledge the women in my own life. Thank you Dinah, Rosamond, Hester and Amanda for your love and inspiration.

JOHN STYLES
London, August 2010

a Boy 6
St Luke old Street
not christened
p
not nursd — Male — Child — old

...LING HOSPITAL — o'Clock

2275

2275 ...ng of the Child

Cap
Biggin
Forehead-Cloth
Head-Cloth
Long-Stay
Bibb
Frock
Upper-Coat
Petticoat
Bodice-Co...
Barrow
Mantle
Sleeves
Blanke...
Neckc...
Roller
Bed
Waist...
Shirt
Clou...
Pilo...
Sto...
Sh...

This Silver Ribbon is
desired to be preserved as
the Childs mark for distinction

...th the Inclosed paper

A Boy
...t Lukes Olde street
not Christened

INTRODUCTION

Fig. 1

A flowered silver ribbon with a paper sewn to it which reads 'This Silver Ribbon is desired to be preserved as the Childs mark for distinction'. Foundling 2275, a boy admitted 6 September 1756

THE LONDON FOUNDLING HOSPITAL was founded by royal charter in 1739. Its work with children has continued uninterrupted to the present day, now carried on by Coram, the modern charity that inherited the Hospital's mission. An unbroken history that stretches across more than two and a half centuries makes it England's longest-established children's charity. The charity has, from the beginning, endeavoured to keep the fullest possible records of the children in its care. Its archive is consequently vast, requiring some 250 metres of shelving for the ledgers and entry books used to record the lives of thousands of forsaken children. Yet even in so large an archive, it comes as a surprise to discover 5,000 small textile items dating from the middle decades of the eighteenth century, pinned to the registration documents that recorded the entry of each baby to the Hospital. These fabrics, retained by the Hospital chiefly as a means of identifying the child with its mother, now comprise the largest collection of everyday textiles surviving from the eighteenth century in Britain. They include the whole range of textile fabrics worn by ordinary women in the mid-eighteenth century, along with ribbons, embroidery and even some baby clothes. Both beautiful and poignant, each scrap of material reflects the life of a single infant child and that of its absent parent.

I. THE FOUNDLING HOSPITAL AND ITS TOKENS

Fig. 2

An exact Representation of the Form and Manner in which Exposed and Deserted young Children are Admitted into the Foundling Hospital (detail), 1749

A mother draws a ball in the ballot for admission to the Hospital, watched by wealthy visitors, including ladies dressed in expensive patterned silks.

THE FOUNDLING HOSPITAL was established 'for the maintenance and education of exposed and deserted young children'. It admitted its first infants in 1741, although the impressive new building on the site of the modern Coram's Fields did not open until 1745 (fig. 3). Initially the Hospital was entirely reliant on private sources of funding – subscriptions, donations and legacies. It rapidly became one of the most fashionable charities in London, at a time when subscription charities were all the rage. Nevertheless, reliance on private funding meant resources were tight. From 1741 to 1756 the Hospital never had enough money to accept all the children brought to its gate, despite its policy of restricting admissions to babies aged two months or less. Intakes of children were limited to one a month or one every two months, with only twenty children – ten girls and ten boys – admitted on each occasion. During these years annual admissions never exceeded 200 children. To ensure fairness, the Hospital instituted a system of selection by ballot in 1742. Women who brought infants to the Hospital drew coloured balls from a bag. A white ball meant the child was admitted, subject to checks for age and infectious disease; a black ball meant rejection (figs. 2, 4, 5). Most were disappointed. Between 1749 and 1756, for example, only 803 babies were accepted out of 2,808 brought to the Hospital. Nearly three-quarters were turned away.

This period of selective entry came to an end in 1756, when Parliament agreed to fund the Hospital on condition that it accepted every child, irrespective of the day it was brought. The following year the maximum age was raised, first to six months and then to twelve. The result was an explosion in the numbers of children

A View of the FOUNDLING HOSPITAL.   Vûe d'HOSPITAL des ENFANS TROUVES.

Published 1st May 1794 by LAURIE & WHITTLE, 53 Fleet Street, London.

Fig. 3

A View of the Foundling Hospital, originally published in 1750

The building was demolished in 1926.

admitted to the Hospital. During the entire fifteen years of selective entry from 1741 to 1756, the Hospital had taken in only 1,384 children. During the four years of the government-funded 'General Reception', between 1756 and 1760, it accepted 14,934, over ten times as many. Annual admissions leapt from under 200 to approximately 4,000, with over a hundred babies arriving weekly during the Spring, when admissions were most numerous.

The contrast between the period of selective entry and the General Reception was not simply a matter of numbers, but also of geography. Before 1756 the vast majority of the Hospital's children came from London. Between 1756 and 1760, almost half came from outside the capital, some from as far afield as Cornwall, Northumberland and north Wales. There was also a change in the circumstances under which they arrived. During the General Reception years, more and more of the children were sent by parish officials across England and Wales. This development may indicate that parents in far-flung parts of the country could not transport their children to the Hospital in London without official assistance. Alternatively, it may indicate the dawning realization by parish officials that, under the liberal admission regime of the General Reception, they could make use of the Hospital to relieve parish ratepayers of the expense of bringing up bastard children. It is important to stress, however, that by no means all the children admitted to the Foundling Hospital at this period were illegitimate, despite statements to that effect made repeatedly at the time and since. During the General Reception, it is likely that as many as a third had married parents, obliged by hardship or separation to give up their offspring in the hope that the Hospital would offer better opportunities in life. Hardship and separation were, of course, even more grinding for the unmarried parents of Foundling children. Both sets of parents were drawn overwhelmingly from the ranks of the labouring poor.

Throughout the period from 1741 to 1760, the process of giving over an infant to the Hospital was an anonymous one. It was a form of adoption, whereby the Hospital became the infant's parent and its previous identity was effaced. Initially no questions at all were asked of those who brought the children to the Hospital, in order to avoid the shame which might otherwise encourage mothers to dump their babies in the streets or even kill them. No record of the mother's name was kept by the Hospital's clerks. Recording the mother's name began only after 1760, when Parliament withdrew its financial support in response to unexpectedly high costs, accusations of mismanagement, and worries about encouraging vice and illegitimacy. Without government funding, the number of places available to deserted children plummeted. A new selection system had to be instituted using petitions, which normally named the mother.

Although admission to the Hospital before 1760 was anonymous, the mother retained the right to reclaim the child if her circumstances changed. In practice such cases were few. Only 152 children were reclaimed out of the 16,282 admitted between 1741 and 1760. This is a tiny number, but it has to be set against the horrifyingly high death rate among babies in the care of the Hospital. Two-thirds of those admitted during these years died. Death rates were especially high for

Fig. 4

*An exact Representation of the
Form and Manner in which
Exposed and Deserted young
Children are Admitted into the
Foundling Hospital* (detail), 1749

This downcast mother has
drawn a black ball. Her child
will not be admitted.

those admitted during the General Reception, when the Hospital was
overwhelmed with babies. Shocking though these figures are, we
should remember that close to half the babies born in London died in
infancy. Infant mortality was appallingly high in most eighteenth-
century cities, where densely packed populations and poor sanitation
encouraged infection. The poverty, hunger and disease that impelled
many mothers to turn to the Foundling Hospital left their babies
particularly vulnerable.

The number of children actually reclaimed by their mothers may
have been tiny, but ensuring that mothers were able to take their
children back was an important priority for the Hospital. From the
start, each baby left in its care was registered with a number,
accompanied by information designed to assist future identification.

Fig. 5

An exact Representation of the Form and Manner in which Exposed and Deserted young Children are Admitted into the Foundling Hospital (detail), 1749

This gratified mother has drawn a white ball. Her child will be admitted.

On the printed registration forms or billets, there were headings for entering the sex of the child, the clothes it was wearing on admission (which were then replaced with Hospital issue), and any special distinguishing marks on its body. In addition, the Hospital encouraged mothers to supply a token, which might be a note, a letter, or a small object, to be kept with the billet as an identifier. Small objects were especially suitable when the mother concerned was illiterate, as so many of the Foundling mothers must have been in the mid-eighteenth century. In 1745, the Hospital emphasized that 'if any particular Marks, Writing or other thing shall be left with the Child, great care will be taken for the preservation thereof'. Mothers were well aware of this (fig. 6). A letter left at the Hospital with a child in 1756 reported 'it is wrote over the Door to have a token sent

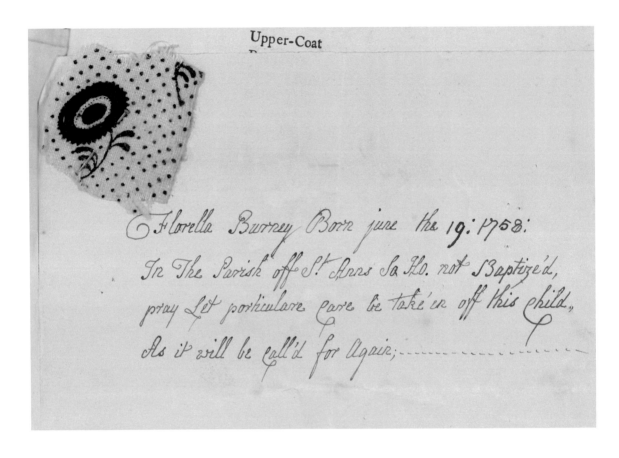

Fig. 6
Linen or cotton printed with dots and red flowers.
Foundling no. 8959. A girl admitted 19 June 1758. The note
says: 'Florella Burney Born june the 19: 1758: In The Parish
off St. Anns SoHo. not Baptize'd, pray Let partiuclare Care
be Taken'en off this Child, As it will be call'd for Again ...'

Fig. 7
A padlock and key left with babies as tokens at the London Foundling Hospital, 1741–60

with the Children for distinction'. By the end of the General Reception in 1760 the practice of supplying tokens had become so familiar that for the next four decades some mothers continued the practice, even though under the petitioning system it was no longer necessary for identifying the child with the mother.

Despite the Hospital's instructions, most of the babies admitted before 1760 arrived without a token. Did the mother simply relinquish any hope of reclaiming her child, or was she too troubled or disorganized? We cannot know. Nevertheless, a small material object survives as an identifier for about 5,000 of the children accepted between 1741 and 1760. Some 200 of these tokens were removed for display at the Foundling Hospital in the middle of the nineteenth century, when the billets, which had originally been folded up with the tokens inside, were flattened for binding into the ledgers now known as the billet books. This group of tokens remains on permanent display in cases at the Foundling Museum in London. It consists not of textiles, but of small items such as metal watch seals, coral necklaces, coins, brooches, rings, padlocks, keys and buttons (fig. 7). As examples of small, everyday objects owned by the kind of poor women who left their babies at the Hospital they are fascinating. Yet these trinkets are entirely unrepresentative of the generality of tokens attached to the billets. They were probably removed for display precisely because they were three-dimensional and too bulky to interleave in bound volumes.

The overwhelming majority of the objects attached to the billets are swatches of textiles. Sometimes, especially during the period from 1741 to 1756, when only selected children were admitted, these pieces of fabric were supplied as a token by whoever left the child, often with an accompanying letter or statement. At other times, especially during the General Reception of 1756 to 1760, when the Hospital was overwhelmed with babies, they were cut, presumably by officials desperate for a ready means of identification, from one of the items of clothing the baby wore when it arrived, such as a sleeve, a ribbon, or most frequently a gown. These textile tokens remain inter-leaved in the billet books. They and the stories they tell about manufacturing, fashion, women's skills, childrearing and maternal emotion are at the heart of *Threads of Feeling*.

DL

Clo

Ribbons

2. TEXTILES

THE SWATCHES in the Foundling Hospital billet books are Britain's largest collection of everyday eighteenth-century textiles, amounting to some 5,000 individual items. They are heavily skewed towards patterned and colourful fabrics, because their purpose was to identify a child. Nevertheless, the collection is so large that it also includes examples of most of the plain, mundane fabrics that we know from other sources to have been worn by ordinary women. The Hospital's clerks often named the cloths. This combination of object and text is unique. Indeed, the Foundling textiles are the only source we have to identify many of the ordinary eighteenth-century textiles whose names we find in written records – Irish stuff and hooping cloth, tinsel and gauze. Above all, they show us the look and feel of the new, colourful printed cottons and linens worn by ordinary women on the eve of the Industrial Revolution. The 1740s and 1750s were critical decades for the expansion of the popular market for printed fabrics, a key stimulus to the famous mechanical inventions that were about to revolutionize the cotton industry, notably James Hargreaves' spinning jenny of 1764 and Richard Arkwright's spinning frame of 1768.

The most striking feature of the Foundling textiles is the sheer number of different types of cloth that passed through the hands of the poor women who left their babies at the Hospital during the twenty years from 1741 to 1760. There are more than 40 different named fabrics, in addition to many others that are unnamed and remain unidentified. Named fabrics include some, like calico, flannel, gingham and satin, that can still be found on the shelves of modern department stores, although the relationship between the eighteenth-

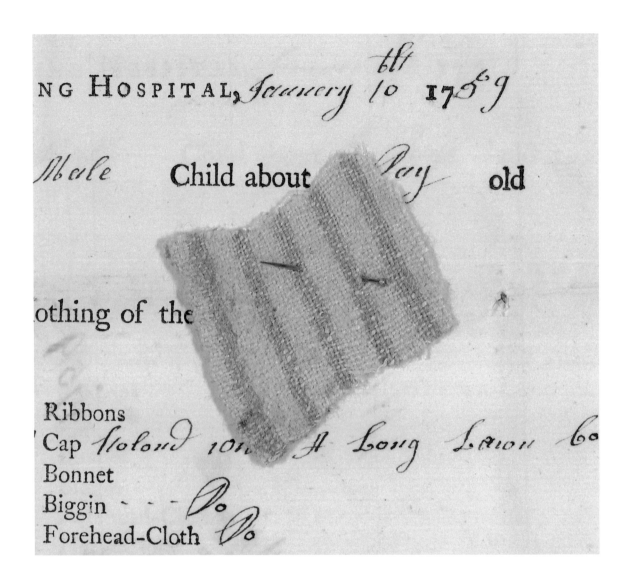

NG HOSPITAL, *January* 10 175⁶9

Male Child about *Pay* old

othing of the

Ribbons
Cap *Holond* 10n *A Long Lawn* 6o
Bonnet
Biggin - - - *Do*
Forehead-Cloth *Do*

Fig. 9

'Striped flannel'. Foundling 11146, a boy admitted 10 January 1759

century fabric and its modern equivalent often turns out to be tenuous in the extreme (figs. 9, 10). Other Foundling textiles boast names utterly mysterious to the modern shopper, exposing a lost world of camblet and fustian, susy and cherryderry, calimanco and linsey-woolsey (fig. 11). When a mid-eighteenth-century provincial shop selling inexpensive textiles might stock only 30 named fabrics, the presence of so many among the Foundling tokens is impressive. It demonstrates that, even before the Industrial Revolution, poor people had access to a colourful range of textiles. These textiles were

Fig. 10

'For a Blanket a Peas of Striped Satten': striped satin. Foundling 13429, a girl admitted 14 July 1759

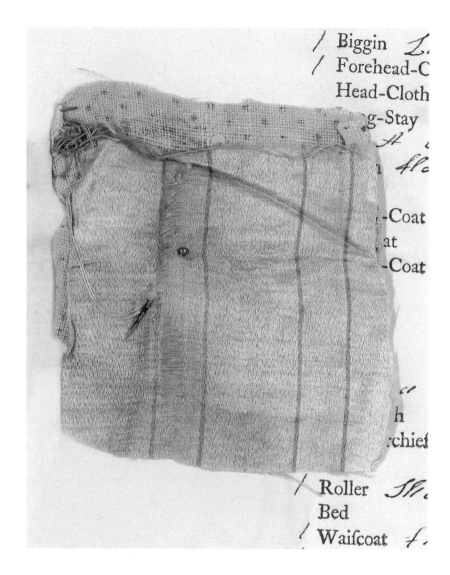

spun and woven by hand, but the spinners and weavers mostly worked for wages. Manufacture and supply was emphatically commercial. All these fabrics could be bought in shops in London and beyond. The mothers who brought fabrics to the Foundling Hospital with their babies either purchased them new, acquired them second-hand, or received them as gifts.

The Foundling textiles include not only a huge variety of different types of fabric, but also fabrics that range in value from the very cheap to the extremely costly. We find textiles like Russia cloth and

Fig. 11

'Red lincey overcast with Purpel Worsted': red linsey-woolsey
embroidered with purple worsted thread. Foundling 13624, a
girl admitted 7 August 1759

Fig. 12

'Brown linen'. Foundling 13298,
a boy admitted 2 July 1759

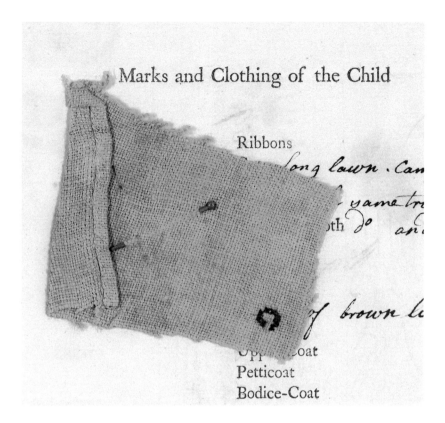

Marks and Clothing of the Child

Ribbons

ong lawn . Can

yame tr

th do and

of brown li

...oat
Petticoat
Bodice-Coat

brown linen, which cost a shilling a yard or less (fig. 12). We know
from parish account books that they were among the cheapest
textiles bought by parish overseers of the poor to clothe paupers.
A little more pricey, at between one and two shillings a yard, were
coarse serges, shalloons, bays and camblets, inexpensive worsted
cloths, often made into working garments for poor women (figs. 13, 14).
Similar in price were linen check, used for aprons, and linsey-
woolsey, a combination of linen and wool, much used for petticoats
(figs. 15, 16). More expensive again, at two shillings a yard or more,
but still widely affordable, were colourful printed cottons and linens,
including a few Indian chintzes (figs. 17, 18). Silk fabrics, however,
were far more costly. The cheapest patterned silks cost five or six
shillings a yard, while ultra-fashionable Spitalfields dress silks woven
in exquisite patterns and worn by grand ladies were more expensive
still. Nevertheless, a handful of silk fabrics can be found among the
Foundling textiles (figs. 19, 20).

Fig. 13

'Blue sarge': blue serge.
Foundling 14522, a girl admitted
19 November 1759

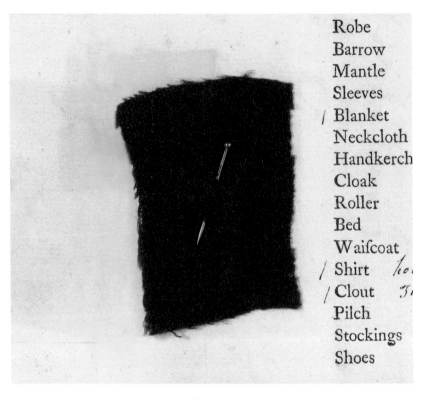

Robe
Barrow
Mantle
Sleeves
/ Blanket
Neckcloth
Handkerch
Cloak
Roller
Bed
Waiſcoat
/ Shirt   *ho*
/ Clout   *3*
Pilch
Stockings
Shoes

Fig. 14

'Blew Camblett': blue camblet.
Foundling 15287, a boy
admitted 26 January 1760

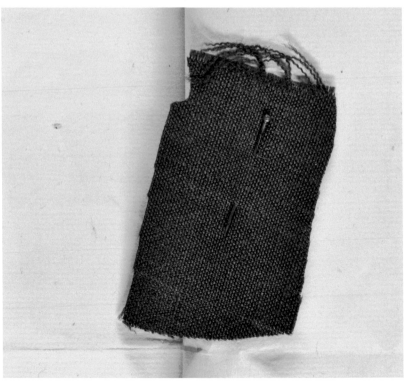

Fig. 15

'Check': linen or cotton woven in a blue and white check pattern. Foundling 13169, a boy admitted 18 June 1759

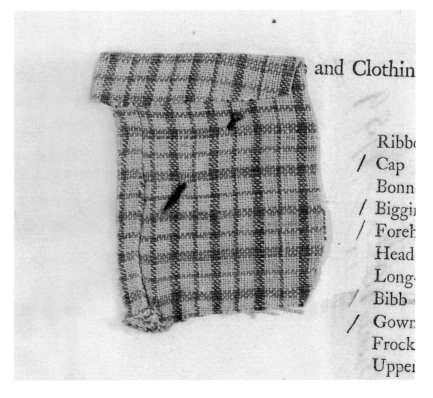

and Clothin

Ribbo
/ Cap
Bonn
/ Biggi
/ Foreh
Head
Long-
/ Bibb
/ Gown
Frock
Upper

Fig. 16

'Striped Linsey': linsey-woolsey woven in blue and white stripes. Foundling 12808, a girl admitted 18 May 1759

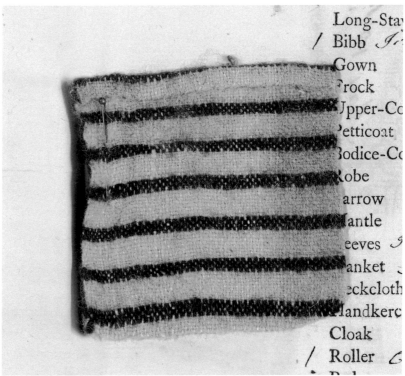

Long-Sta
/ Bibb
Gown
Frock
Upper-Cc
Petticoat
Bodice-Cc
Robe
arrow
Mantle
eeves
anket
eckcloth
Handkerc
Cloak
/ Roller

Fig. 17

'Flowered cotton': cotton printed with flowers. Foundling 374,
a girl admitted 18 December 1747

Fig. 18

'Flowered chince': chintz. Foundling 13789, a girl admitted 27
August 1759

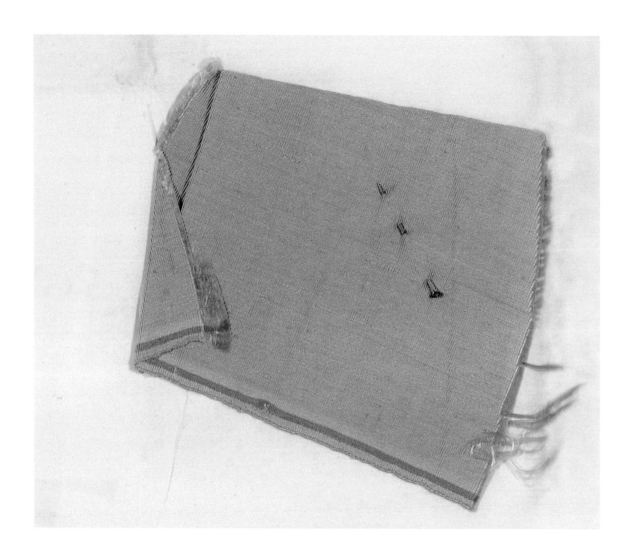

Fig. 19
'A piece of blue silk pin'd on ye
Breast'. Foundling 1254, a girl
admitted 29 May 1755

It is cheaper fabrics that account for the vast bulk of the clothing textiles in the Foundling Hospital billet books, but not the very cheapest. The majority consist of the moderately expensive printed cottons and linens. Stripes and checks woven in linen or cotton are the next most common category. The remainder, a small minority, consists of a variety of disparate fabrics – woollens, worsteds, linens, cottons, silks. It is not surprising that printed cottons and linens predominate. They offered the kind of distinctive, colourful patterns crucial for memorable identification and yet they were cheap enough for many mothers to acquire them. Most of the printed cottons and linens in the Foundling archive were actually cut from

On the fabric, handwritten: *border* ... *plaine bo...*

Fig. 20

'Flowered silk': a brocaded silk, probably of the 1740s.
Foundling 15023, a girl admitted 3 January 1760

the babies' clothing, but we should remember that clothes worn by poor infants at this period were customarily made out of discarded adult garments, often the mother's. It is for this reason that the Foundling textiles include so few of the heavy, dark fabrics – kerseys, fustians, thicksets, corduroys – worn by men. It was working women who wore the moderately expensive yet affordable printed linens and cottons so common among the Foundling textiles, often as their best gowns. These colourful printed fabrics provide, therefore, a unique opportunity to observe how ordinary young women engaged with fashion.

3. FASHION

Fig. 21

'Purpel Red and blue white flowered': cotton or linen printed with red and blue flowers and dots. Foundling 10579, a boy admitted 11 November 1758

IN THE MID-EIGHTEENTH CENTURY, the silk fabrics woven with complex, colourful patterns for women's gowns at Lyon in France and Spitalfields in London were the pinnacle of élite fashion (fig. 22). The gown itself was the key fashion garment for both rich and poor, the largest and most expensive decorated item in most women's wardrobes. But silks were costly. They were also virtually impossible to wash, indeed difficult to clean at all. Their cost and their impracticality put them beyond the reach of most ordinary women. Unable to acquire silk gowns, poorer women turned increasingly in the 1740s and 1750s to printed linens and cottons, which offered new

Fig. 22

A court mantua made from a cream tabby brocaded silk, woven at Spitalfields, 1759–62 (detail)

Fig. 23

'Silk. Fringe': an expensive flowered dress silk of about 1750, with a matching piece of fly braid. Foundling 2584, a girl admitted 27 October 1756

Fig. 24

'Flowerd cotten': cotton printed with flowers. Foundling
14093, a girl admitted 4 October 1759

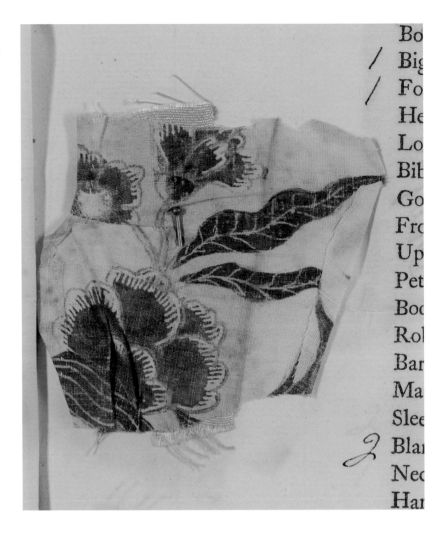

Fig. 25
'Chins': chintz. Foundling 13414,
a girl admitted 13 July 1759

ways to dress fashionably. Cotton and linen prints incorporated key elements of the fashionable look of the far more expensive flowered silks. They may not have matched the silks for sheen, delicacy and vibrancy of colour, but they could mimic their colour combinations and designs at a fraction of the cost (figs. 23, 24). In addition, their fast colours meant they could be washed.

Printing in fast colours on light textiles was a novelty. The technique originated in India. Brightly coloured Indian cotton chintzes had been imported to England in large numbers in the later seventeenth century, but were then banned because of the threat they posed to English-made textiles. Imports of cotton textiles from

Fig. 26

'Flowered lining': linen printed with flowers and leaves. Foundling 12924, a girl admitted 26 May 1759

Bed
Waifcoat *Pinper*
Shirt *Irish bound*
Clout *mslien*
Pilch
Stockings
Shoes

Marks on

A g

not Christened

India collapsed, although small quantities continued to be smuggled (fig. 25). However, by the time the ban was imposed, manufacturers in the British Isles had already started to copy the Indian technique, adapting it to linen and later developing new kinds of printing (figs. 26, 27, 28). By the 1740s and 1750s, British-made printed textiles were dominating the market for women's gowns.

Precisely what attracted ordinary consumers to cotton and linen prints becomes clearer if we compare them to the alternatives. Before the introduction of printed linens and cottons, poorer women had to make do with cheap light woollens and worsteds such as camblet, calimanco and stuff for their best gowns. Some of these fabrics can be found among the Foundling textiles. Though often attractively patterned, they tend to be densely coloured, in predominantly dark shades (figs. 29, 30). The bright cream or white grounds of the cotton and linen prints are almost entirely missing. It was the light grounds of the cottons and linens that gave them the clean look so prized for gowns because it mimicked the fashionable silks of the period. In the

Fig. 27

'Flowered lawn': flowers printed on lawn, one of the finest
linens. Foundling 11868, a girl admitted 4 March 1759

ing of the

ibbons

ap *Irish*

onnet

iggin *Plain*

orehead-Cloth

ead-Cloth

ng-Stay

b

wn *Flower*

ock

Upper-Coat

Petticoat

Bodice-Coat

Robe

Fig. 28

'Flowered lining': linen printed with flowers using the
copperplate printing technique introduced by Francis Nixon
near Dublin in Ireland in 1752. Foundling 11877, a boy admitted
5 March 1759

Fig. 29

'Striped Calimanker':
calimanco, a worsted cloth,
woven in stripes and figures.
Foundling 12956, a girl admitted
30 May 1759

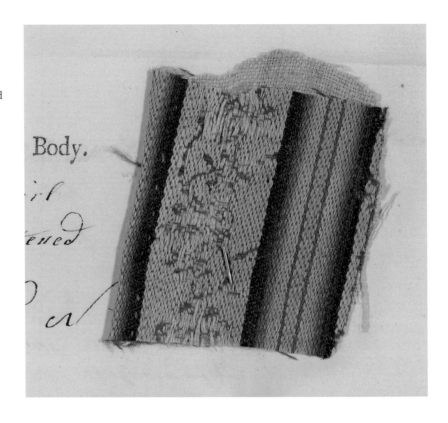

Fig. 30

'Stript stuff': worsted stuff
striped purple and green.
Foundling 14629, a boy
admitted 29 November 1759

1740s and 1750s, these prints cost rather more than their woollen and worsted rivals, but they still outsold them. It is no coincidence that when a Covent Garden linen draper's servant wanted to give presents to a girl in 1758, it was printed cotton for her gowns that he stole from his master.

What we see when we examine the printed fabrics among the Foundling textiles is a democratization of fashion. Textile printing gave poorer women colourful designs which overlapped in aesthetic effect with the fashionable silks worn by their wealthy sisters, even when worn as a short bedgown which needed less material than a full-length gown (fig. 31). It is unlikely these printed textiles were ever mistaken for fine silks, but there was a generic resemblance in colour and design. This was true even of the cheapest, coarsest printed fabrics, which account for most of those in the Foundling Hospital billet books. The majority of the Foundling printed textiles are executed in a single colour, which was cheaper to print. Many of them make extensive use of dots produced by nails hammered into

Fig. 31

John Collet, *The Female Orators*, 1768 (detail)

A female street seller is depicted wearing a short bedgown with a sprigged pattern on a cream or yellow ground, probably intended to suggest a printed linen or cotton.

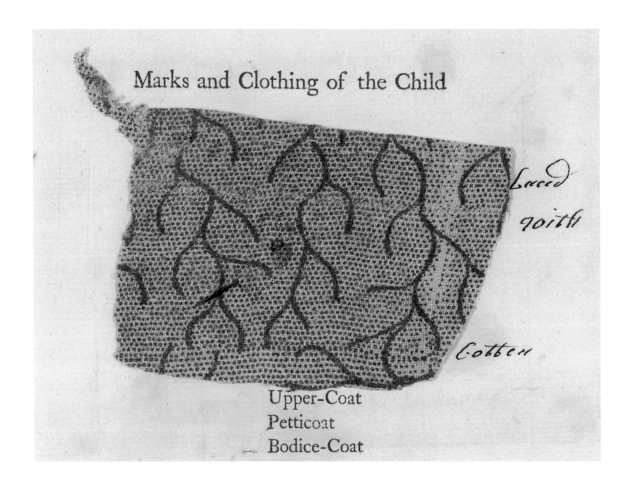

Marks and Clothing of the Child

Laced
goith

Cotten

Upper-Coat
Petticoat
Bodice-Coat

Fig. 32

'Spriged cotten': cotton printed with sprigs and dots. Foundling 13287, a boy admitted 30 June 1759

the wooden printing block, one of the most economical methods of patterning a block (fig. 32) Yet even simple, monochrome designs of this kind, though sometimes crudely executed, could sustain a fashionably Rococo effect, with designs featuring botanically-inspired sprigs or shell forms (fig. 33). Even among these simple prints, the range of variation is remarkable. It is rare for the same pattern to recur among the hundreds of different printed designs found in the Foundling textiles. Evidently, the choice of cheap printed fabrics available to consumers in the mid-eighteenth century was immense.

Fig. 33

'Blue and white sheled': cotton or linen printed with a blue and white shell pattern. Foundling 11148, a girl admitted 11 January 1759

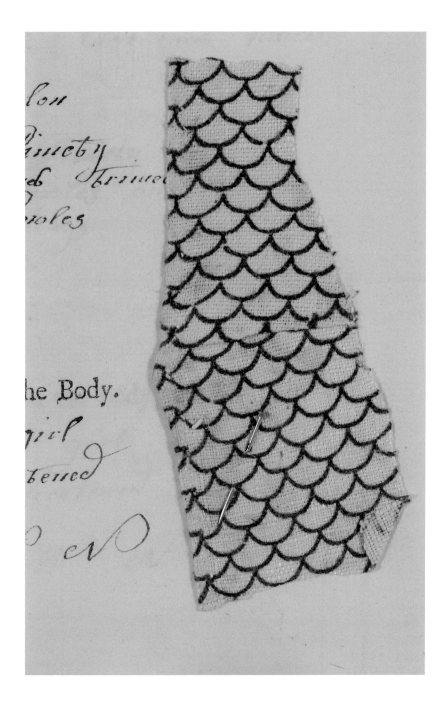

4. RIBBONS

Fig. 34

'The Inclosed Ribbon tyed on ye right wrist': a flowered silk ribbon. Foundling 1293, a boy admitted 9 August 1755

FASHION IN THE EIGHTEENTH CENTURY was never simply a matter of the cloth from which garments were made. Accessorizing was crucial. No accessory was more versatile than ribbons, which decorated women's hats, sleeves, gowns, and, above all, the white linen caps all women wore indoors. Advocates of plain dress were ever alert to the seductive allure of ribbons, like the Quakers in 1762 who lambasted 'the present prevailing fashion in the extravagant use of ribbands which too many of our youth especially have fallen into about their hats'.

Usually made from silk, the most prized and costly material, ribbons added luxury and colour in an inexpensive manner (figs. 34, 35). A yard of multicoloured figured ribbon in bright, lustrous tints could be purchased for a few pence. Plain ribbons were cheaper still. The variety of colours and patterns on sale was enormous. Cheap, colourful, patterned and diverse: these characteristics made ribbons perfect identifiers for Foundling babies. They account for nearly a third of the Foundling textiles.

Yet there was more to the link between ribbons and the Foundling babies than vibrant colours and varied patterns. Ribbons were the very currency of romance, love and courtship, especially in their role as fairings, the gifts exchanged between lovers at fairs and holidays. The late seventeenth-century ballad, 'Faint Heart never won fair Lady', advised young men to:

Win her with Fairings and sweetening Treats,
Lasses are soonest o'recome this way;
Ribbons and Rings will work most strange feats,
and bring you into favour and play.

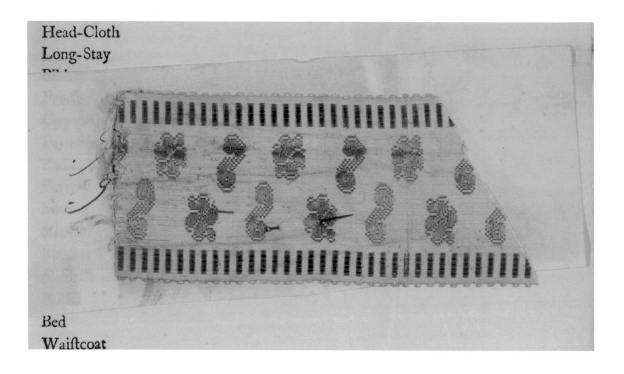

Head-Cloth
Long-Stay

Bed
Waiſtcoat

Fig. 35

'With ye Inclosed Paper pin'd on ye Breast and ye Inclosed Ribbon under it': a flowered silk ribbon. Foundling 1177, a boy admitted 26 January 1755

Fig. 36

O Dear! What can the Matter be?, 1793

The man carries a hat decorated with ribbons in his left hand.

The worried lover in the eighteenth-century song, 'O Dear! What can the Matter be?', waits anxiously for her Johnny to return from the fair (fig. 36).

> He promis'd to buy me a pair of blue stockings,
> A pair of blue garters that cost him but two pence,
> He promis'd to bring me a bunch of blue ribbons,
> To tie up my bonny brown hair.

As the song suggests, ribbons in favourite colours were worn by sweethearts as material emblems of attachment. Their emotional significance was especially strong when the beloved was absent. The emotion could be rendered more intense by tying the ribbon in knots, known as loveknots, defined by Samuel Johnson in 1755 in his famous dictionary as 'A complicated figure, by which affection interchanged is figured' (figs. 37, 38). The effect could be intensified yet further by attaching other love tokens, such as coins or rings, to the ribbon, hanging it round the neck, or tying it to an item of clothing for greater intimacy.

O DEAR! what can the MATTER BE

Publish'd July 20. 1793. by C. Sheppard.

N.º 15, St Peters Hill, Doctors Commons.

1

O Dear! what can the matter be?
Dear, dear! what can the matter be?
O Dear. what can the matter be.
Johnny's so long at the fair.
He promis'd to buy me a pair of blue stockings,
A pair of new garters that cost him but twopence,
He promis'd to bring me a bunch of blue ribbons,
To tie up my bonny brown hair.

2

O Dear. what can the matter be?
Dear, dear! what can the matter be?
O dear what can the matter be.
Johnny's so long at the fair:

He promis'd to bring me a basket of posies.
A garland of lillies. a garland of roses,
A little straw hat to set off the blue ribbons,
That tie up my bonny brown hair.

3

O dear, see how he's runing,
O dear see he's a coming,
Dear! dear: see how he's runing,
Johnny's return'd from the fair:
He's brought me a delicate basket of posies,
A garland of lillies, a garland of roses,
A little straw hat to set off the blue ribbons,
To tie up my bonny brown hair.

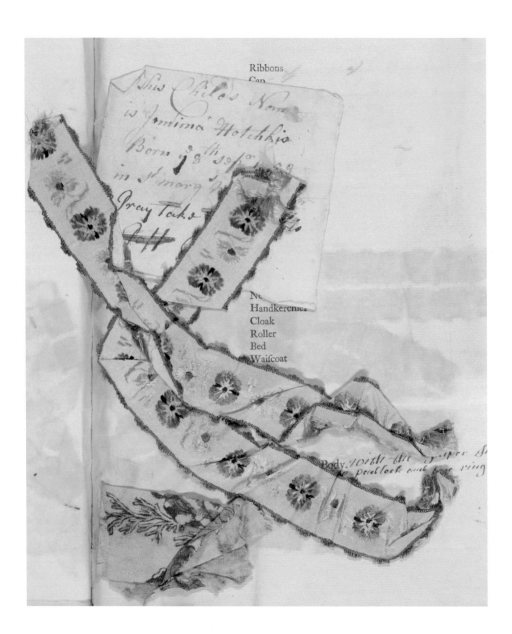

Fig. 37

A flowered silk ribbon, knotted. Foundling 10667, a girl
admitted 29 November 1758

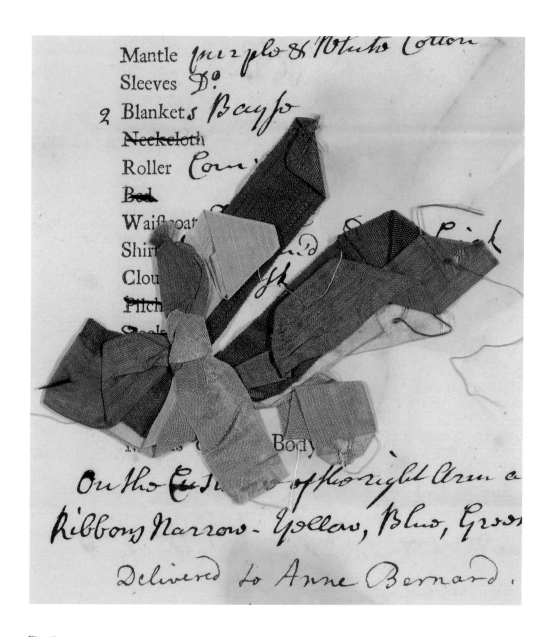

Fig. 38

'A bunch of 4 ribbons narrow – Yellow, Blue, Green, & Pink':
silk ribbons tied in a bunch with a knot. Foundling 170, a girl
admitted 9 December 1743

Of course, romance and courtship did not necessarily lead to marriage. A stock character in eighteenth-century ballads was the young woman courted at the fair with tokens of love and promises of marriage who falls pregnant only to be deserted by her lover. It must have been a common enough experience among the mothers who left their illegitimate babies at the Foundling Hospital. The verses left with her baby by one such mother in 1759 express her powerful sense of male betrayal.

> Hard is my Lot in deep Distress
> To have no help where Most should find
> Sure Nature meant her sacred Laws
> Should men as strong as Women bind

One reason that ribbons served as powerful tokens of mothers' love for the babies left at the Foundling Hospital was, therefore, because they were universally recognized symbols of love, especially in circumstances of separation and loss. Another reason ribbons were employed in this way was because eighteenth-century mothers commonly used the ribbons they attached to their babies' caps to distinguish between girls and boys. There is no evidence in the Foundling textiles of the kind of colour coding of clothes by the baby's sex that is so familiar today. Pink is as likely to be the colour of a Foundling token left with a boy as with a girl. It was not the colour of the ribbons sewn to the babies' caps that distinguished girls from boys, but their form. Ribbons attached to girls' caps always took the form of what was called 'a topknot', a loose bunch of knotted ribbon with strands hanging down. Ribbons attached to boys' caps, by contrast, were always in the form of a cockade, a neatly formed circular rosette (figs. 41, 42). The difference arose almost certainly from the military and therefore masculine associations of the cockade. Eighteenth-century soldiers' uniforms usually included tricorn hats with cockades in the national colours attached. For most British soldiers in the mid-eighteenth century the cockades were black, the Hanoverian colour (fig. 39). The boy babies who arrived at the Foundling Hospital wore cockades in a wide variety of colours. There is no evidence that the colours of their cockades had any

particular significance, but wearing a cockade rather than a topknot evidently did. The arrangement of the ribbons testified to the sex of children too young to be differentiated by their garments (fig. 40).

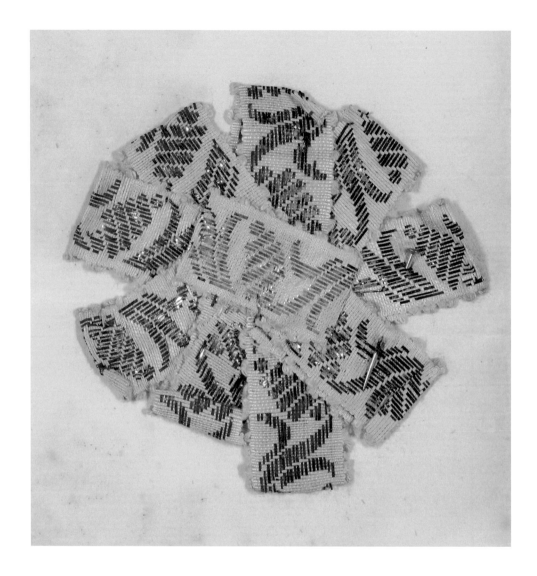

Fig. 41

'A White and Silver Cockade': a cockade made from tinsel
ribbon. Foundling 728, a boy admitted 6 April 1751

Fig. 42

'A black Cockade on his head': a cockade made from black silk
ribbon. Foundling 208, a boy admitted 22 February 1745

FOUNDLING·HOSPITAL, *June* 30 1753 at *12* o'Clock

Letter *I a Male* Child about *a fortnight* old

Marks and Cloathing of the Child

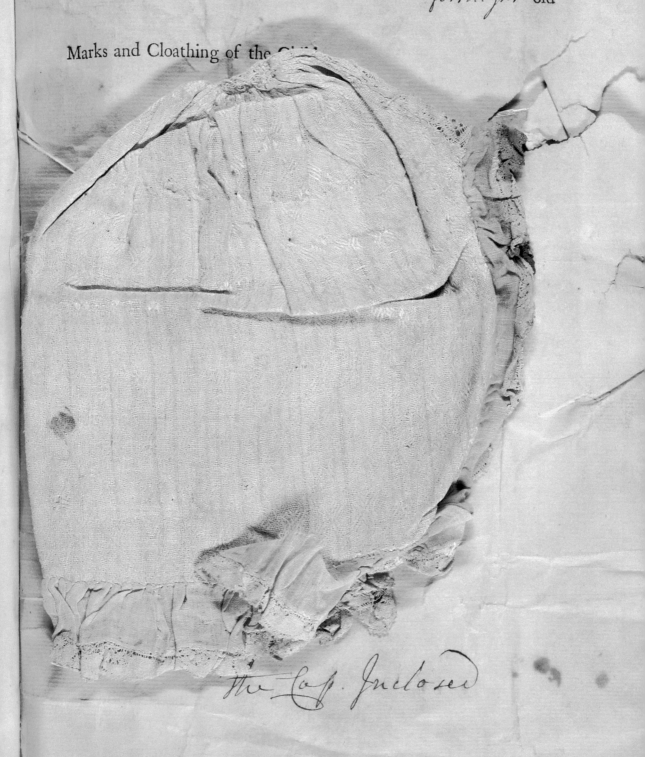

the Cap. Inclosed

5. BABY CLOTHES

Topknots and cockades are not the only pieces of infant clothing that survive intact in the Foundling Hospital records. For a handful of the children, the token consists of a complete sleeve, cap, or other infant garment. Sleeves are the most numerous (figs. 45, 46). These were separate, pull-on items, worn when the child's body was wrapped in bands of fabric called rollers, or dressed in a looser, long wrapping garment with armholes called a mantle (fig. 44). The sleeves left as tokens were especially elaborate, with cuffs in a different fabric to the rest of the garment, carefully chosen to co-ordinate in terms of colour and design. Often the mothers who left these sleeves as tokens must also have made them. Impoverished and desperate they may have been, but these sleeves show they did not lack aesthetic discrimination when it came to adorning their babies. The poor did not live in black and white.

Fig. 44

William Hogarth, *The Enraged Musician* (detail), 1741

A ballad singer holds a baby in her arms dressed in a bag-like wrapper, with separate sleeves.

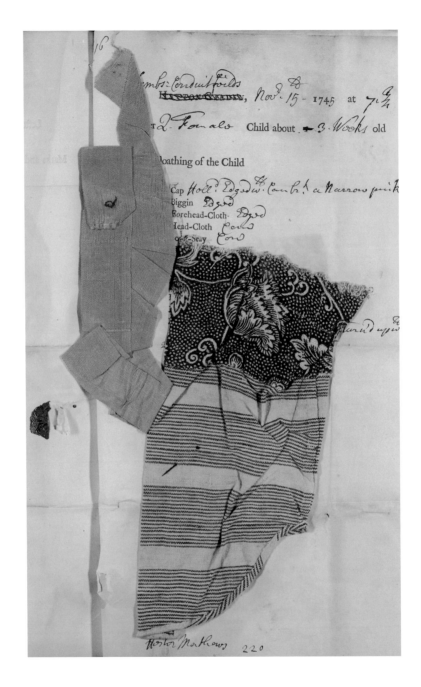

Fig. 45

'Sleeve blue and white strip'd cotton turn'd up with purple
and white linen': a baby's sleeve made from cotton woven in
stripes, with a cuff made from linen printed with flowers.
Alongside is 'a narrow pink'd Ribbon' in silk. Foundling 220, a
girl admitted 15 November 1745

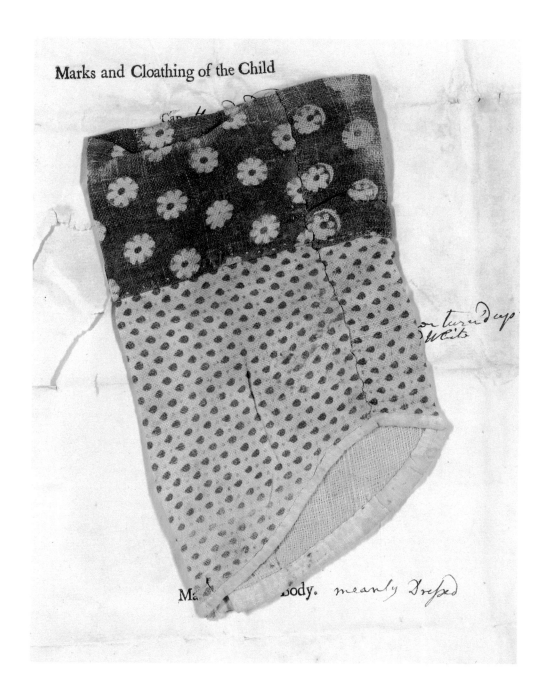

Fig. 46

'Sleeves red and white speckl'd linen turn'd up red spotted
with white': a baby's sleeve made from linen printed with red
dots, with a cuff of cotton or linen printed in red with white
flowers. Foundling 235, a boy admitted 23 May 1746

Letter G *male*   Child about *forteene days* old

Sr please to admit this
child in Bobliced

g6971

Marks on the Body.

6. NEEDLEWORK

Fig. 47

An embroidered sampler.
Foundling 14695, a boy
admitted 6 December 1759

THE PATTERNED, COLOURFUL FABRICS that comprise the bulk of the Foundling textiles were generally printed or woven, and commercially sourced. There was, however, another technique for decorating fabrics that was in widespread use in the eighteenth century – embroidery. A great deal of embroidery was produced commercially for sale and, in London especially, huge numbers of poor women scraped a living working in the needle trades (fig. 48). At the same time, eighteenth-century women were expected to sew for their families, which might involve decorative in addition to utilitarian needlework, even among the poor. For mothers of Foundling babies who possessed the necessary skills, the needle offered an unrivalled means of personalizing the textiles they left as tokens.

A wide range of what can loosely be termed embroidery techniques can be found among the Foundling textiles, including satin stitch, chain stitch, crewel work, patchwork, blackwork, quilting and Dorset buttons. There are numerous examples of what is probably professional decorative embroidery, much of it in silk, although we should not assume that a piece of embroidery was professionally sewn simply because it is accomplished (fig. 49). The Foundling textiles also include many examples of what is clearly non-professional embroidery, often executed in woollen or worsted yarn. What this crude embroidery lacks in skill is sometimes offset by its raw emotional power (fig. 50). Nevertheless, much of it is so rudimentary that it is almost impossible to decipher its meaning, even if it has one (fig. 51). Sometimes these crude stitches may simply be the marks that women sewed on garments to identify them when they were washed communally or stolen.

Fig. 48

The Seamstress, 1765

The presence of so much extremely crude decorative sewing among the Foundling textiles raises the possibility that needle skills were not so universal among working women as has often been assumed. Needlework was undoubtedly considered an important female skill. Young working women seeking employment as domestic servants were often expected to know how to sew. Yet many girls, especially in the countryside, were taught spinning and knitting rather than sewing because they provided better

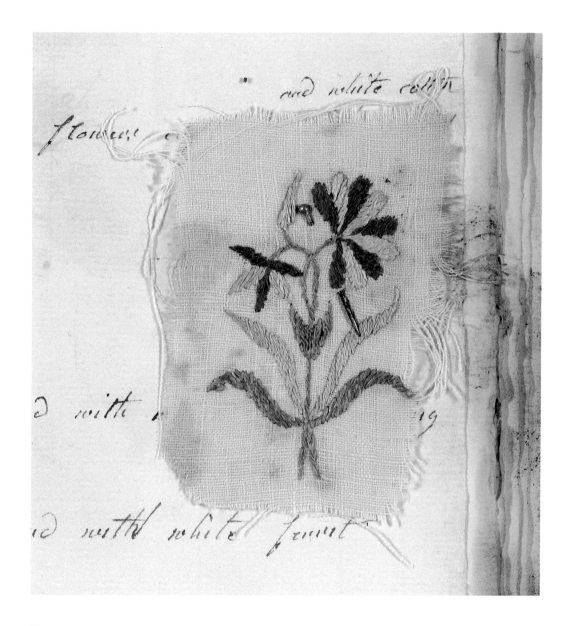

Fig. 49

'Worckt with flowers': linen or cotton embroidered with
flowers. Foundling 14084, boy admitted 3 October 1759

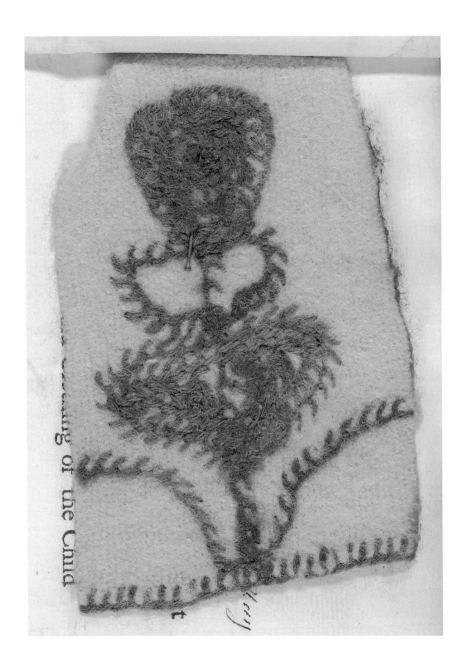

Fig. 50

'Flannel the bottom worked': flannel embroidered in worsted
thread with a flower. Foundling 12843, a boy admitted 19 May 1759

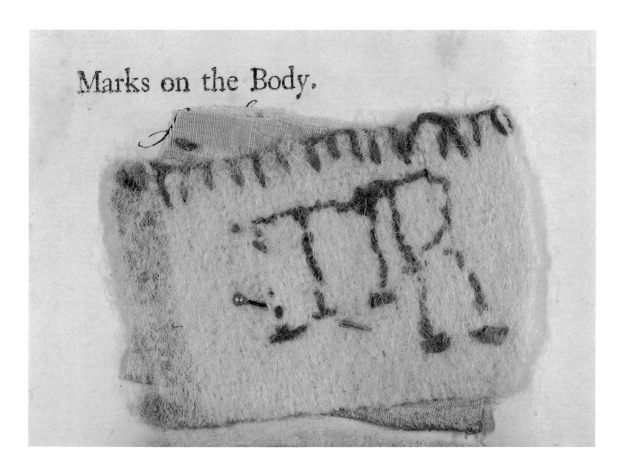

Fig. 51
'Flannel marked M R and overcast with red worsted': white flannel embroidered in red worsted thread. Foundling 11285, a boy admitted 22 January 1759

opportunities for employment. Later in the eighteenth century, a survey of the poor of Chester found that, in one parish, three-quarters of girls aged 9 to 13 'could not sew at all, and not one of them so well as to make a single article of dress'. Even in London, there were those like Esther Hudson, a street seller in 1785, who when asked if she could make basic garments, replied 'No, I never makes nothing'. Many mothers of Foundling babies might have said the same. The Foundling textiles suggest that one of our key stereotypes of eighteenth-century women may be wrong.

a Long Lawn Border

Bour

B cmck ioll

7. MOTHERS AND BABIES

Fig. 52
'The Bit of Red Cloth Enclosed was pined to the Childs Cap': a heart cut from red woollen cloth, a ribbon of blue paduasoy silk, and a piece of linen diaper. Foundling 10563, a girl admitted 22 November 1758

THE FOUNDLING TEXTILES present us with a concrete connection to both individual Foundling babies and the mothers who renounced them. The only other information we have about most of them is whatever is contained in the anonymous, formulaic words of the billet and its accompanying Hospital records. Examining the textiles pinned to the billets – tangible evidence of babies forsaken, many destined to die within a few days or weeks – is overwhelming and sobering.

We must remember, however, that for most of the babies there was never a token. Even where a small piece of fabric is pinned to the billet, it is more likely to have been chosen by the Hospital's officials for administrative convenience during the General Reception than by the mother as testimony of maternal separation and loss. Many Foundling babies were simply dumped at the Hospital, uncared for and unloved. A boy admitted in 1757 was described as 'Clothed with Rags Swarming with Varmen'. Another admitted a few months later was 'A Mear Skilinton Covered with Rags with a hole in the Roofe of the Mouth'. Yet another in 1759 was reported to have been 'exposed and deserted by the parents of the sd child or persons unknown and left to the mercy of the world'.

It would be all too easy to interpret these examples of ill-treatment as evidence that the eighteenth-century poor made little emotional investment in their babies, because infants were a drain on family resources and were likely to die young – the view of an earlier generation of historians. It would, however, be wrong. There have always been newborns who were unloved, abused and carelessly abandoned. The presence of the unwanted among the Foundling babies is hardly surprising. The Hospital was set up specifically to cater for them and the terms of the General Reception encouraged their admission. Nevertheless, alongside examples of heartless desertion, the Foundling textiles offer numerous expressions of maternal love, hope, yearning and remorse.

The continuing attachment of mothers to the babies they were giving up to the Hospital is evident in their efforts to name them. Although it must have been common knowledge that the Hospital gave the babies new names, mothers constantly asserted their own choice of name, or, at the very least, tried to register a clue to their baby's original identity in the Hospital records. Some employed written letters and notes, but others sewed names, initials, birth dates and birthplaces on fabric, or even wrote them on ribbons (figs. 53, 54). It is as if for these poor women, many of them barely literate or ill at ease with a pen, spelling out precious information on cloth rendered it personal, tangible and permanent in a way mere ink on paper could never do. Even the most crudely sewn initials seem to have conveyed a special kind of intimacy, sustaining the child's individual bond with its mother in the face of the institution.

The hopes the mothers invested in their babies were also expressed in fabric. Letters left by mothers suggest that babies were often left at the Hospital in the belief that it offered their child better opportunities in life than they ever could. A mother in 1749 wrote about her infant boy, 'having a most dear and Tender regard for it … I have trusted it to a Charity establish'd upon so good a Foundation as knowing my circumstance will not permit me to take so great a Care of it.' Yet such hopes were expressed far more vividly by means of carefully selected textile images, often obtained by customizing the natural imagery commonly employed in designs printed on linens and cottons. An acorn or a bud might suggest germination and new growth, a bird or a butterfly the chance to fly free, a flower the capacity to blossom and fruit (figs. 55, 56, 57, 58).

Powerful maternal hopes could be embodied in embroidered names and natural imagery, but the most direct expressions of raw maternal emotion found among the Foundling tokens are those that used the heart, the established symbol of love in the eighteenth

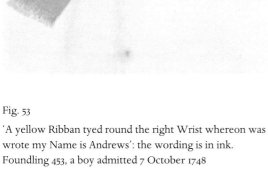

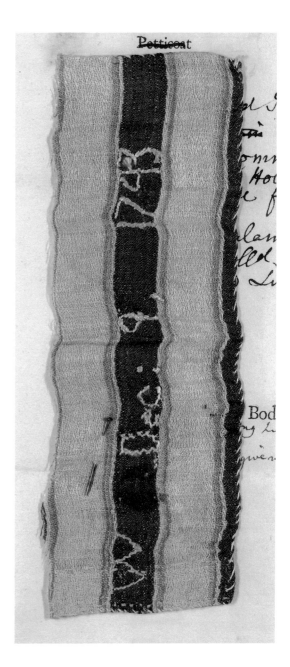

Fig. 53

'A yellow Ribban tyed round the right Wrist whereon was wrote my Name is Andrews': the wording is in ink. Foundling 453, a boy admitted 7 October 1748

Fig. 54

'Strip'd susa mark'd W Dec 9 1743': striped susy, a silk fabric from India embroidered with an initial and a date. Foundling 166, a boy admitted 9 December 1743

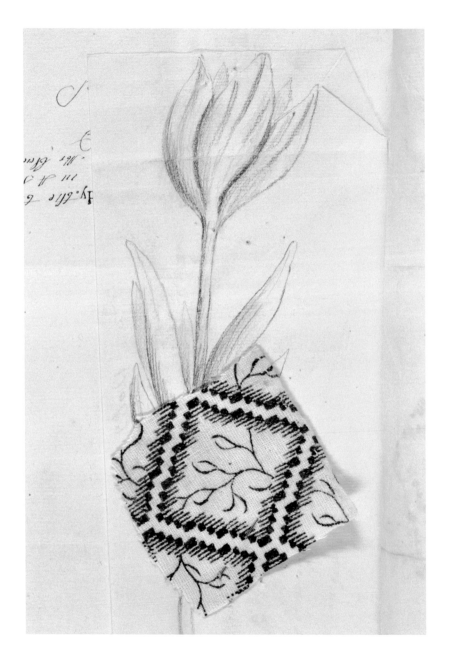

Fig. 55

A drawing of a tulip and a piece of cotton or linen printed
with sprigs and diamonds. Foundling 12052, a girl admitted 18
March 1759

Fig. 56
'Printed calico': calico printed with a bird. Foundling 13476, a
boy admitted 20 June 1759

Fig. 57

Cotton or linen printed with a
butterfly. Foundling 9018, a boy
admitted 23 June 1758

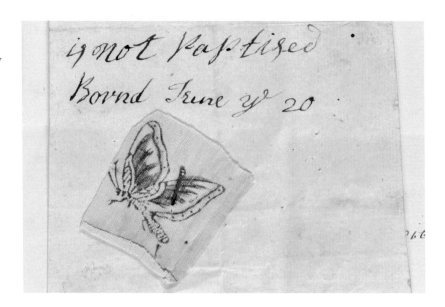

Fig. 58

Cotton or linen printed with an
acorn. Foundling 9324, a boy
admitted 22 July 1758

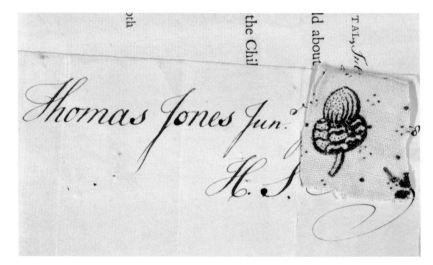

century, as it is today (fig. 52). The heart was believed to be literally
the seat of the emotions. Foundling mothers left suit of hearts playing
cards, hearts drawn on paper, metal hearts, embroidered hearts, hearts
cut out in fabric and even, in the case of one baby boy, a gown printed
with a suit of hearts playing-card pattern (fig. 59). One heart-shaped
metal pendant left as a token carried the lines 'you have my Heart,
Tho' we must Part', but the words seem almost redundant, such was
the familiarity of the heart as an emblem of love.

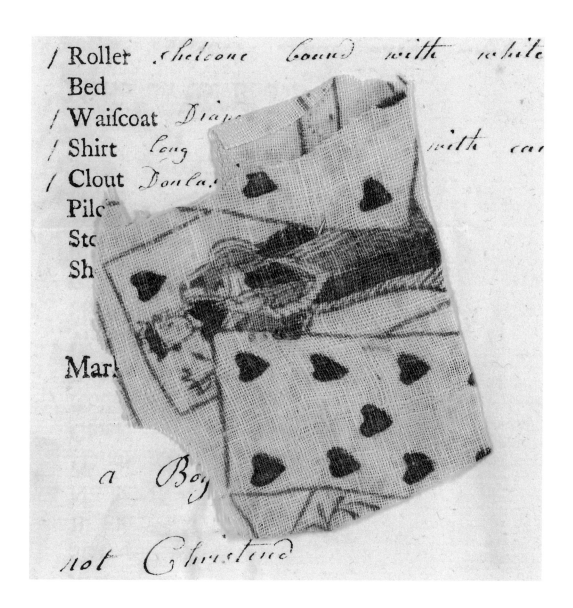

Fig. 59

'Flowered all over with cards': cotton or linen printed with a
playing-card pattern. Foundling 14922, a boy admitted 24
December 1759

CONCLUSION

Fig. 60

A patchwork needlecase made from printed and woven fabrics, embroidered with a heart and the initials SC, and cut in half. Foundling 16516, a boy admitted 11 February 1767. Christened Charles, but given the name Benjamin Twirl by the Hospital. Reclaimed by his mother, Sarah Bender, on 10 June 1775

To a modern audience it can seem odd that the mothers of Foundling babies used cloth to express the most tender human feelings. Of course many of them, probably most, were illiterate. They could only express themselves on paper if their words were written down for them by others. The language of ribbons and hearts, by contrast, was accessible to all. But the mothers' recourse to textiles as a vehicle for self-expression was not just a second-best substitute for writing. Theirs was a world where verbal literacy existed in conjunction with a kind of material literacy that is now much diminished; a world in which the use of certain objects to mark events, express allegiances and forge relationships was familiar and the meaning of those objects widely shared. To us, a small scrap of fabric linking mother and child seems ineffably fragile – surely the thread will snap. It is only occasionally, in those rare moments when it was the agent of reunion between a mother and her Foundling Hospital child, that we glimpse the power it once exercised. It is fitting that the only token illustrated in this book for a child reclaimed by its mother is a piece of patchwork with a heart sewn on it in red thread (fig. 60). It was subsequently cut in half. One half was presented with the child to the Hospital. The other was, presumably, kept by the mother until the reunion, when the heart was made whole.

No. 16516

Male C

Xtned Charles

11 Febry 1767

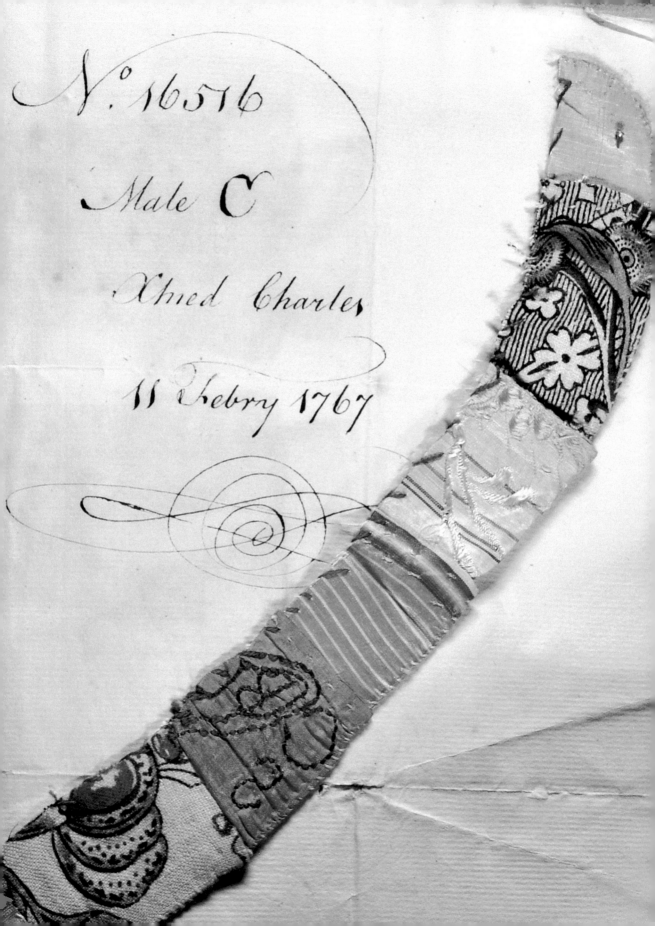

SELECT BIBLIOGRAPHY

Anne Buck, *Clothes and the Child: A Handbook of Children's Dress in England, 1500–1900* (Carlton, 1996)

Gillian Clark, 'Infant Clothing in the Eighteenth Century: A New Insight', *Costume*, 28 (1994), 47–59.

Gillian Clark, 'Infant Fashion in the Eighteenth Century: Evidence from Foundlings Nursed in Berkshire', *The Local Historian*, 29 (1999), 3–13.

Beverly Lemire, *Fashion's Favourite: The Cotton Trade and the Consumer in Britain, 1660–1800* (Oxford, 1991)

Alysa Levene, *Childcare, Health and Mortality at the London Foundling Hospital, 1741–1800: 'Left to the Mercy of the World'* (Manchester, 2007)

Ruth McClure, *Coram's Children: The London Foundling Hospital in the Eighteenth Century* (London and New Haven, Conn., 1981)

Gail Marsh, *Eighteenth-Century Embroidery Techniques* (Lewis, 2006)

Florence Montgomery, *Textiles in America* (London and New York, 1984)

R.H. Nichols, and F A. Wray, *The History of the Foundling Hospital* (London, 1935)

John Styles, *The Dress of the People: Everyday Fashion in Eighteenth-Century England* (London and New Haven, Conn., 2007)